NFL TODAY

THE STORY OF THE
PITTSBURGH STEELERS

NFL TODAY

THE STORY OF THE PITTSBURGH STEELERS

JOHN NICHOLS

CREATIVE EDUCATION

Cover: Quarterback Ben Roethlisberger (top),
defensive tackle Joe Greene (bottom)
Page 2: Wide receiver Hines Ward
Pages 4–5: Banner of linebacker Jack Lambert
Pages 6–7: Defensive end L. C. Greenwood

....

Published by Creative Education
P.O. Box 227, Mankato, Minnesota 56002
Creative Education is an imprint of
The Creative Company
www.thecreativecompany.us

Design and production by Blue Design
Design Associate: Sarah Yakawonis
Printed by Corporate Graphics
in the United States of America

Photographs by Corbis (Bettmann, Gary C. Caskey/
epa, Jason Cohn/Reuters, John G. Mabanglo/epa),
Getty Images (Morris Berman/NFL, Alan Copson,
David Drapkin, Michael Fabus, Focus On Sport,
George Gojkovich, John Iacono/Sports Illustrated,
Ross Lewis/NFL, Andy Lyons, NFL, Jim McIsaac, Peter
Read Miller/Sports Illustrated, Darryl Norenberg/
NFL, Pro Football Hall Of Fame/NFL, Robert Riger,
Manny Rubio/NFL, Gregory Shamus, Paul Spinelli,
Thomas E. Witte)

Library of Congress Cataloging-in-Publication Data

Nichols, John, 1966-.
The story of the Pittsburgh Steelers / by John
Nichols.
p. cm. — (NFL today)
Includes index.
ISBN 978-1-58341-767-6
1. Pittsburgh Steelers (Football team)—History—
Juvenile literature. I. Title. II. Series.

GV956.P57N53 2009
796.332'64'0974886—dc22   2008022698

CPSIA: 121510 PO1414
9 8 7 6 5 4 3

CONTENTS

ON THE SIDELINES

MEET THE STEELERS

STRUGGLES IN STEEL CITY

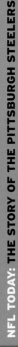

Known as "The Steel City" due to its manufacturing tradition, Pittsburgh is also sometimes called "The City of Bridges" because of the many crossings over its three big rivers.

Pittsburgh, Pennsylvania, was founded at the junction of three rivers. The waters of the Allegheny, Monongahela, and Ohio rivers have served as Pittsburgh's economic lifeblood since its first settlers used them to ship their harvests to market in the early 1700s. In 1901, the United States Steel Corporation was founded in Pittsburgh, and for decades, the city produced the steel used to build a growing nation. Today, modern Pittsburgh still embraces the industrial roots that make it America's "Steel City," but it has also grown to become one of the nation's leaders in the fields of health care, banking, and robotics.

In 1933, a local businessman named Arthur "Art" Rooney bought Pittsburgh a franchise in the National Football League (NFL). Initially named the Pirates, after Pittsburgh's major league baseball team, Rooney eventually changed the name to the Steelers in honor of the city's hard-working citizens. Nearly 80 years later, the Steelers remain the pride of Pittsburgh and one of the NFL's most storied franchises.

Art Rooney's Pirates would eventually experience great success, but initially, wins were difficult to come by. The club posted a 3–6–2 record its first season in 1933 and finished last in the NFL's Eastern Division. Pittsburgh's struggles would continue, and the Pirates' 6–6 mark in 1936 represented

the best record the franchise would post during the 1930s.
Despite the losses, fans saw some strong performances by
such players as Hall of Fame running backs Byron "Whizzer"
White, who led the NFL in rushing in 1938, and Johnny "Blood"
McNally, who returned his first kick for Pittsburgh 92 yards for
a touchdown. But despite their efforts, the Pirates spent the
decade at the bottom of the standings.

In 1940, Rooney changed the team's name from Pirates
to Steelers. The change in name didn't produce better results
on the field, however, as Pittsburgh sputtered to a 2–7–2
record. "I want the team to represent the city of Pittsburgh,"
said a disappointed Rooney. "I think the people of Pittsburgh
deserve a little better than that."

The Steelers finally experienced some success in 1942
under head coach Walt Kiesling. A Hall of Fame lineman on
both sides of the ball as a player, Kiesling finished out his
playing career with Pittsburgh in 1938 before taking over as
coach the following season. Kiesling's 1942 Steelers rode the
strong legs of rookie running back "Bullet" Bill Dudley, who
led the league in rushing with 696 yards, to post a 7–4 record.
It was the franchise's first winning mark. By 1943, many NFL
players—including Dudley—had left football to serve in World
War II. That season, Pittsburgh merged with the Philadelphia

ART ROONEY

TEAM OWNER
STEELERS SEASONS: 1933-88

A lifelong Pittsburgh resident, Art Rooney grew up in a working-class family and never forgot his roots. Despite accumulating great wealth during his lifetime, Rooney kept his home in the same Pittsburgh neighborhood he had lived in since the 1930s. In 1933, Rooney purchased the Steelers franchise for $2,500—part of his winnings from betting on horses during one lucky weekend at New York's Saratoga Race Course. Rooney's luck then seemed to run cold as the Steelers suffered through decades of losing football, but his belief that the team would eventually bring a championship to Pittsburgh never wavered. In 1974, during Rooney's 41st season as owner, the Steelers finally rewarded his patience with the first of six Super Bowl titles. (Rooney lived long enough to see only four of those triumphs.) Known as "The Chief," Rooney was loved by fans, players, and coaches alike. "Mr. Rooney made everyone he met feel special," said Steelers running back Franco Harris. "Whether you sold popcorn at the stadium or were the star of the team, he treated everyone with kindness and dignity."

ON THE SIDELINES

RETIRED NUMBER

In the long history of the Pittsburgh Steelers, only one player has ever had the honor of having his number retired—defensive tackle Ernie Stautner (who wore number 70). Stautner's 14-year career during the 1950s and early '60s spanned a period when the Steelers were perennial losers, but no one doubted the greatness of Stautner. At 6-foot-1 and 230 pounds, Stautner was a small lineman, even by the standards of his time, but what he lacked in size, he more than made up for with bearish strength and burning desire. A nine-time Pro-Bowler, Stautner's ferocity and never-say-die attitude made him a folk hero among Pittsburgh's blue-collar fans. After retiring Stautner's number, the Steelers made a decision not to retire any others in the future. While none have officially been set aside, many numbers used by the team's 1970s greats have not been reissued to new players. One player in the early 1980s was temporarily given Hall of Fame linebacker Jack Ham's number 59 but was later stripped of it by the team's equipment manager because, as the manager said, "that kid wasn't Jack Ham."

Eagles to form one team. In their one season together, the "Steagles" went 5–4–1. The next year, the still short-handed Steelers merged with the Chicago Cardinals and posted a dismal 0–10 record. After the war ended in 1945, many of the players returned home, and Pittsburgh was able to field its own team again. But despite the efforts of all-time NFL greats such as Dudley and defensive tackle Ernie Stautner, the Steelers enjoyed only two winning seasons between 1944 and 1956.

In 1957, the Steelers hired former Detroit Lions coach Ray "Buddy" Parker to lead the team. After Pittsburgh went just 6–6 in 1957, Coach Parker made a trade to obtain his former quarterback from Detroit—Bobby Layne. Layne was a tough and confident leader whose will to win often outshone his average athletic ability. "As bad as he looked throwing the ball, he was a winner," said San Francisco 49ers head coach Howard "Red" Hickey. "You'd work him out and you wouldn't want him, but you'd want him in your huddle."

To further boost his offense, Coach Parker then struck a trade with the Detroit Lions in 1960, bringing running back John Henry Johnson to Pittsburgh. The move turned out to be a smart one, as the bull-strong, 210-pound Johnson would rush for more than 4,300 yards during his 6 seasons in

X At 6-foot-6 and 280 pounds, Steelers standout John Baker was one of the NFL's largest and hardest-hitting defensive ends in the 1960s.

Pittsburgh—numbers that eventually helped him earn a place in the Pro Football Hall of Fame.

The Steelers posted four winning records in their next eight seasons. They made their strongest bid for the playoffs in 1962, when they went 9–5 and finished just behind the New York Giants in the NFL's Eastern Conference. After the season, the 36-year-old Layne retired, and the Steelers were suddenly struck by tragedy when defensive tackle Gene "Big Daddy" Lipscomb died of a drug overdose prior to the 1963 season. With the losses of their veteran leaders, things quickly went downhill in Pittsburgh. It would be nearly a decade before the Steelers enjoyed another winning season.

CHUCK NOLL

COACH
STEELERS SEASONS: 1969-91

Chuck Noll is credited with taking one of the NFL's worst franchises and turning it into a dynasty. During his 23 seasons as head coach of the Steelers, Noll's teams won 4 Super Bowl titles and 9 division titles, and made 12 playoff appearances. Noll's strength was in identifying and developing talent. Nine of the players he drafted during his tenure went on to be inducted into the Pro Football Hall of Fame. Noll was a strong believer in fundamental football, and his players were always sure of their assignments and rarely made mental mistakes. Noll is credited with being a great teacher of the game. When a Steelers player would make a mistake, Noll would not scream or yell or embarrass the player; instead, he would pull him aside, ask him what he saw, and then give him instruction on how to correctly make the play the next time. Noll's reserved personality and disdain for the limelight often caused him to be overlooked among his peers, but his record speaks for itself. Noll was enshrined in the Hall of Fame in 1993.

BUILDING THROUGH THE DRAFT

X-------------------------------

X In a 13-year Pittsburgh career that ran from the 1960s to the '80s, tall and frighteningly fast defensive end L. C. Greenwood helped make the Steelers defense a juggernaut.

In 1969, former Baltimore Colts assistant coach Chuck Noll was named Pittsburgh's new head coach. A patient leader, the 37-year-old Noll knew that the best way to build a real "team of steel" in Pittsburgh would be through the NFL Draft. The new coach made his first big move in 1969 by drafting 6-foot-4 and 275-pound defensive tackle Joe Greene from little-known North Texas State. As a first-year player, Greene quickly earned the respect and admiration of his teammates. "Joe came in to camp his rookie year and hit everything in sight," said Steelers center Ray Mansfield. "We offensive linemen were glad when the season started so he could go beat up on somebody else for a change."

It didn't take long for Greene to make his mark on the rest of the league as well. His size, speed, and intensity made him equally effective at both stopping the running game and rushing the passer. Greene would team with another 1969 draft pick—defensive end L. C. Greenwood—to anchor a mighty defense that became known as the "Steel Curtain."

X Joe Greene was as unselfish as he was dominant; he would often willingly engage two blockers in order to free up his fellow defensive linemen.

But despite the additions of the two defensive stalwarts, the Steelers went just 1–13 in 1969.

In 1970, the Steelers moved into a brand-new home. Three Rivers Stadium, with its 59,000 seats, represented a major upgrade for the Steelers and their fans after decades of playing at Forbes Field and the University of Pittsburgh's Pitt Stadium. Looking also to upgrade the team's offense, the Steelers added a new quarterback. With the first overall

X The bigger the game, the better running back Franco Harris seemed to play, showing rare versatility as a ballcarrier, blocker, and receiver.

ROCKY BLEIER'S COMEBACK

Running back Robert "Rocky" Bleier was not the most talented member of the powerhouse Steelers teams of the 1970s, but no one would argue that he wasn't the most courageous. Following his rookie season in Pittsburgh, Bleier was drafted into the U.S. Army and sent to the Vietnam War in 1969, where he was seriously injured. A gunshot wound to his left leg and grenade shrapnel that tore up his right leg and foot sent him to the hospital for several months. Upon returning home, Bleier had to learn how to walk again. Over the next three years, Bleier rebuilt his body, never giving up on his dream of returning to the Steelers. In 1974, that dream came true when Bleier finally began to see regular playing time. By 1976, he and Franco Harris became only the second running back tandem in NFL history to rush for 1,000 yards apiece. By the time Bleier retired in 1980, he was a four-time Super Bowl champion. "My story is like the story of a lot of veterans," said Bleier. "We didn't want our dreams to end in the war."

pick in the 1970 NFL Draft, Noll selected Terry Bradshaw, a strong-armed star from Louisiana Tech University. Despite his talent, Bradshaw struggled his first year, throwing only 6 touchdowns against 24 interceptions. But bolstered by their blossoming defense, the Steelers improved to 5–9. By 1972, Noll had added more talent to the roster, drafting linebacker Jack Ham (1971) and running back Franco Harris (1972).

The young Steelers squad finally began to flex its muscles in 1972. After suffering through eight straight losing seasons, Pittsburgh roared to an 11–3 record, winning the American Football Conference (AFC) Central Division and making the playoffs. Harris led the way by rushing for more than 100 yards in 6 straight games, tying an NFL record. "Franco was the key man on our ballclub," Greene later noted. "We were coming on every year in the 1970s. All we needed was the catalyst, and Franco was it."

The resurgent Steelers made their first appearance in the playoffs since 1947. In the first round, Pittsburgh rode a last-second, 60-yard touchdown catch and gallop from Harris to defeat the Oakland Raiders 13–7. In the AFC Championship Game, the Steelers claimed an early lead, but with Bradshaw sidelined for most of the game with a concussion, Pittsburgh fell to the Miami Dolphins 21–17.

PITTSBURGH'S
SUPER STEELERS

In 1973, the Steelers rolled to a 10–4 record and another playoff berth. Once again, the team's strongest suit was its defense. Five members of the Steel Curtain, including linebacker Andy Russell and defensive end Dwight White, were named to the Pro Bowl, but it was clear that the team still lacked a championship-caliber offense. After a disappointing 33–14 first-round playoff loss to Oakland, Noll again turned to the draft for help.

The coach's sharp eye for talent helped Pittsburgh strike gold once more. Noll's choices of wide receivers Lynn Swann and John Stallworth, center Mike Webster, and linebacker Jack Lambert in the 1974 Draft represent what many football experts consider to be the best one-year draft haul in NFL history. All four would eventually be inducted into the Pro Football Hall of Fame, and their contributions would fuel the Steelers' leap to greatness.

Bolstered by their super rookies, the 1974 Steelers ended owner Art Rooney's 41-year wait for a championship. After

Center Mike Webster combined brains and brawn to become a Hall-of-Famer; an honor student at the University of Wisconsin, he became known as one of the strongest men in the NFL. **X**

JOE GREENE

DEFENSIVE TACKLE
STEELERS SEASONS: 1969-81
HEIGHT: 6-FOOT-4
WEIGHT: 275 POUNDS

One of the greatest defensive linemen ever to play the game, Joe Greene's rare combination of power, speed, and agility made him an unstoppable force in the middle of the Steelers' defense. Mild-mannered and reserved off the field, the 6-foot-4 and 275-pound tackle was so fierce on the field that he earned the nickname "Mean Joe" Greene. The Steelers' first-round pick in 1969, Greene was the first piece and eventual anchor of what would become the famous "Steel Curtain" defense, consistently drawing and defeating two blockers on every play. Greene's dominance was on full display during one particularly outstanding game in 1972 against the Houston Oilers. In that game, Greene recorded five quarterback sacks, blocked a field goal, and forced and recovered a fumble to lead the Steelers to a key victory. A passionate leader, Greene's spirited play helped lift the Steelers out of a decades-long cycle of losing to become the NFL's premier team of the 1970s. The 10-time Pro-Bowler and 5-time All-Pro selection was elected to the Hall of Fame in 1987.

posting a 10–3–1 record in the regular season, Pittsburgh thrashed the Buffalo Bills and Oakland Raiders en route to a Super Bowl IX matchup with the Minnesota Vikings. Backed by a suffocating defense and Franco Harris's 158 yards rushing, the Steelers smothered the Vikings 16–6 to claim their first NFL championship. "Today's win made all the other years worth it," said an emotional Rooney. "I am happy for the coaches and players, but I'm especially happy for the Pittsburgh fans. They deserved this."

Pittsburgh fans remained happy in 1975 as the Steelers won 11 straight games in the course of a 12–2 regular season. The defense continued to dominate, led by cornerback Mel Blount's 11 interceptions, and the offense was sparked by the acrobatic Swann's 11 touchdown catches. After dispatching the Baltimore Colts and Raiders in the playoffs, the Steelers faced the Dallas Cowboys in Super Bowl X. Bradshaw's 64-yard fourth-quarter touchdown bomb to Swann became the decisive play in a 21–17 Pittsburgh victory.

The next two seasons saw the Steelers come up short in their pursuit of a third championship. But just when many thought Pittsburgh was at the end of its reign, the Steelers cemented their legacy as the "Team of the '70s" by winning two more Super Bowls. In 1978, they went 14–2 and topped

ON THE SIDELINES

THE IMMACULATE RECEPTION

For nearly four decades, luck was not a friend to the Pittsburgh Steelers. The team was a consistent loser, and it seemed that every bad break that could happen did. Facing the powerful Oakland Raiders in a 1972 playoff game at Three Rivers Stadium, fate seemed ready to deliver another cruel blow to the Steelers as they trailed 7–6 with only 22 seconds left in the game. Desperate for a big play, quarterback Terry Bradshaw heaved a long pass toward running back John "Frenchy" Fuqua. Just as the ball was approaching Fuqua's hands, Raiders safety Jack Tatum collided with Fuqua, knocking the ball several yards backward in the air. Out of nowhere, a hustling Franco Harris caught the ball just before it hit the ground and raced to the end zone to score the winning touchdown. The 60-yard score was so miraculous that it became known as the "Immaculate Reception." Pittsburgh's championship run ended soon after that game, but Harris's improbable play signaled the beginning of what would become an unstoppable dynasty in the 1970s.

X Mel Blount (with ball) was widely regarded as the "prototype" cornerback in the 1970s, a tall, fast, powerful ballhawk with a knack for returning the football after his 57 career interceptions.

the Cowboys 35–31 in Super Bowl XIII. A year later, the

Steelers went 12–4 during the regular season and crushed

the Los Angeles Rams 31–19 in Super Bowl XIV. In contrast

to the team's first two Super Bowl wins, in which the Steel

Curtain defense carried the day, Pittsburgh's second two

titles showcased its powerful offense. Bradshaw's strong arm,

Harris's determined running, and the fleet feet of Swann and

Stallworth gave Pittsburgh an attack just as fearsome as its buzz-saw defense. "Say what you want about the Steelers defense—Steel Curtain and all that—they deserve every bit of it," said Houston Oilers coach O. A. "Bum" Phillips. "But they got all those weapons on offense that nobody talks about. They can move it as good as anybody, and that's why they got all those rings."

Blessed with effortless speed and the jumping ability of a basketball player, Lynn Swann posted 124 receiving yards to help Pittsburgh overwhelm Dallas in Super Bowl XIII. **X**

RETIRING THE OLD GUARD

As the Steelers entered the 1980s, the accomplished members of the Team of the '70s started retiring one by one. After a couple of mediocre seasons to start the decade, Pittsburgh rose up again to reach the 1984 AFC Championship Game. The team had rebuilt around young talents such as rookie receiver Louis Lipps and linebacker Mike Merriweather, but the Steelers' jarring 45–28 conference title game loss to the Miami Dolphins left them short of the Super Bowl.

The Steelers struggled through the mid-1980s, and one of the few bright spots for the team was the play of John Stallworth, one of the remaining stars from the 1970s. The silky-smooth Stallworth played most of his career in the shadow of the more flamboyant Swann, but his quiet greatness came forward during the '80s. In 1984, at age 32, Stallworth caught 80 passes—11 of which were for touchdowns—to earn his fourth trip to the Pro Bowl.

X By the end of his playing days, John Stallworth (number 82) owned nearly every Pittsburgh receiving record, including career catches (573) and receiving touchdowns (63).

Following Stallworth's retirement in 1988, the Steelers finished the decade with one more playoff appearance. In 1989, quarterback Walter "Bubby" Brister led Pittsburgh to a 9–7 record and a first-round playoff win over the Houston Oilers. The season ended the next week, though, with a 24–23 loss to the Denver Broncos. After missing the playoffs in both 1990 and 1991, Coach Noll decided to call it quits. The man

TERRY BRADSHAW

QUARTERBACK
STEELERS SEASONS: 1970–83
HEIGHT: 6-FOOT-3
WEIGHT: 215 POUNDS

Few people would have predicted stardom for Terry Bradshaw after his first two seasons in the NFL. The former first-round draft pick struggled mightily as a young quarterback on a bad team, and many fans and experts questioned his intelligence and talent. But Bradshaw proved them all wrong. After taking some early lumps, Bradshaw grew to become one of the best big-game quarterbacks in NFL history. Blessed with a powerful arm and a flair for the big play, the Louisiana native was one of the last NFL quarterbacks to exclusively call his own plays. A two-time recipient of the Super Bowl's Most Valuable Player (MVP) award, Bradshaw's finest championship effort came in Super Bowl XIII, after the 1978 season, when he threw for 318 yards and 4 touchdowns in Pittsburgh's 35–31 victory over the Dallas Cowboys. A three-time Pro-Bowler, Bradshaw was voted the NFL's MVP in 1978 and was elected to the Hall of Fame in 1989. After his playing career ended, Bradshaw successfully moved on to the world of broadcasting, becoming an analyst for the television show *Fox NFL Sunday*.

who had transformed the Steelers from league doormat to
perennial powerhouse retired with a sparkling career record
of 209–156–1. "Coach Noll taught me that being a coach
is really about being a teacher," said Tony Dungy, a former
Steelers player and assistant coach who went on to win the
Super Bowl as head coach of the Indianapolis Colts. "That
was his philosophy, and now it is mine."

To replace the legendary Noll, the Steelers chose
Pittsburgh native Bill Cowher. Like Noll, the 34-year-old
Cowher was considered by many to be too young to be a
head coach. Cowher also shared Noll's conviction that playing
power football, which consisted of a hard-hitting defense

X Known for his
jutting chin and loud
coaching style, Bill
Cowher was a fan
favorite who always
seemed to keep the
Steelers in contention.

and an offense built on a strong running game, was the path that led to championships. A former NFL linebacker, Cowher's intensity and fiery personality were a perfect fit with Pittsburgh's hard-working, blue-collar fans. "I grew up in Pittsburgh. I know Pittsburgh, and I know what Steelers football is all about," said Cowher at his hiring. "We are going to play Steelers football."

Cowher's energy made an immediate impact in 1992, as the Steelers posted an 11–5 record, and Cowher won NFL Coach of the Year honors. Pittsburgh's new group of stars—such as playmaking linebacker Greg Lloyd, speedy cornerback Rod Woodson, sure-handed receiver Yancy Thigpen, and quarterback Neil O'Donnell—helped the Steelers earn six straight playoff berths between 1992 and 1997. In 1995, the high-powered Steelers marched through the playoffs and earned a berth in Super Bowl XXX opposite their old rival, the Cowboys. The game was a tight affair, but Dallas escaped with a 27–17 victory.

The Steelers remained an AFC heavyweight in the seasons that followed. Even though Woodson and several other standouts eventually left, new talent continued to emerge. In 1996, Jerome Bettis—a 5-foot-11 and 250-pound running back nicknamed "The Bus"—rumbled for 1,431 yards.

ONE-SIDED LOGO

For many years, the Steelers did not have an official logo to use on their helmets. The players' headgear was simply one solid color: gold. But in 1962, the team decided to honor the city's steel industry by introducing a new logo based on the one created by the U.S. Steel Corporation. The Steelmark logo featured three hypocycloids (diamond shapes) in a circle around the word "Steelers." The three diamonds initially represented the three-point motto of the company: "Steel lightens your work, brightens your leisure, and widens your world." Later, the colored diamonds were also interpreted to represent the materials used in steel production—yellow for coal, orange for iron ore, and blue for scrap metal. The Steelers first used the logo during the 1962 season. Unsure if fans would approve, owner Art Rooney had the logo put on only the right side of the helmet. The unique look was an instant hit, and the Steelers experienced their best season in years. As a final touch late in the season, the Steelers' helmets were changed from gold to black to better highlight the proud logo.

JACK LAMBERT

LINEBACKER
STEELERS SEASONS: 1974-84
HEIGHT: 6-FOOT-4
WEIGHT: 220 POUNDS

When opposing quarterbacks looked across the line of scrimmage at Pittsburgh's "Steel Curtain" defense, the first thing they were likely to see was middle linebacker Jack Lambert's toothless, intimidating scowl. The hard-hitting Lambert made life difficult for opposing offenses throughout the course of his 11-year career. Fast, ferocious, and relentless, Lambert played with reckless abandon, swallowing up ballcarriers and smacking down receivers. A second-round draft pick from Ohio's Kent State University, the 6-foot-4 and 220-pound Lambert was considered by many to be too small to be an effective linebacker in the NFL. But he quickly laid all doubts to rest when he won the NFL Defensive Rookie of the Year award in 1974. Lambert's rare ability to stuff the run, drop back in coverage, and run from sideline to sideline sometimes made it seem as though he was everywhere at once. "They must have a couple Lamberts, because there's no way one guy did all that," said Cleveland Browns head coach Sam Rutigliano after a 1981 game. A nine-time Pro-Bowler, Lambert was awarded a place in the Hall of Fame in 1990.

In 1997, Kordell Stewart took over at quarterback full-time after dazzling opponents early in his career as a part-time receiver, running back, and quarterback. He led the Steelers to playoff berths in 1997, 2001, and 2002 but could not deliver another championship to Pittsburgh. Stewart left the Steelers after the 2002 season to play for the Chicago Bears, and Pittsburgh struggled to a 6–10 mark under his replacement, Tommy Maddox. "It's awful tough to consistently win in the NFL," said a disappointed Cowher at the close of the season. "We've been good for a long time, but this year we took our lumps. Now that we've been knocked down, the challenge for us all will be to get back up again."

X Even as he lost speed late in his career, running back Jerome Bettis piled up touchdowns as he was used like a battering ram on goal-line plays.

BIG BEN SPARKS THE STEELERS

In the two decades following Pittsburgh's streak of Super Bowl glory in the 1970s, the Steelers consistently fielded good and even great teams, but despite their overall success, they failed to capture another championship. One of the reasons that the Steelers continually came up short was the team's struggle to find a long-term replacement at quarterback for Bradshaw, who had retired in 1983.

In 2004, the Steelers aimed to fill that void by drafting Ben Roethlisberger from Miami University (Ohio) with their first-round pick. "Big Ben," as the 6-foot-5 and 240-pound quarterback came to be known, was an NFL rarity, a rookie quarterback who played well and won big in his first season. Inspired by their talented rookie and other standouts such as wide receiver Hines Ward, safety Troy Polamalu, and linebacker Joey Porter, the Steelers roared to a 15–1 regular-season record. In the playoffs, the Steelers advanced to the AFC Championship Game, but Roethlisberger threw three interceptions as the New England Patriots sealed a 41–27 victory. "I picked a bad time to have a bad game," said Roethlisberger. "I felt like I let a lot of our veteran guys down. After the game, I talked to a bunch of them and asked them to give me another chance."

Roethlisberger got that second chance in 2005 when the

Steelers returned to the playoffs. Behind Roethlisberger's sharp passing, running back Willie Parker's open-field speed, and the Steelers' stout defense, Pittsburgh beat the Bengals, Colts, and Broncos to advance to Super Bowl XL in February 2006. In the title game, Parker's 75-yard gallop for a touchdown and Ward's 43-yard touchdown catch sparked the Steelers to a 21–10 victory over the Seattle Seahawks. "It's an amazing feeling," said Bettis as the Steelers celebrated their fifth Super Bowl championship. "We've been so close before, but now the wait is over. We're the champs!"

Prior to the 2006 season, Roethlisberger was seriously injured in a motorcycle accident. Although the young quarterback recovered to start the season on time, his accident seemed to be a bad omen for what proved to be a frustrating season for the defending champions. After stumbling to a 2–6 start, the Steelers rallied behind Parker's 1,494 rushing yards to win 6 of their last 8 games and finish 8–8. The roller-coaster season convinced Cowher that it was time to step down after 15 seasons at the helm.

To replace Cowher, the Steelers hired fiery young coach Mike Tomlin. The 35-year-old defensive coordinator came from the Minnesota Vikings, where, in one year, he had managed to turn the Vikings into one of the league's top defenses.

TERRIBLE TOWELS

Prior to a 1975 playoff game against the Baltimore Colts, Steelers broadcaster Myron Cope was looking for a way to get the already loud Pittsburgh fans even more interested and involved. Cope's idea was for fans to bring "lucky" yellow towels to the stadium on game day. For a week before the game, Cope reminded his audiences to bring their "terrible towels" to the game to wave and "drive the Steelers to superhuman performance." Many people, including several Steelers players, disliked the idea, but on game day, some 30,000 Terrible Towels waved in the stands, inspiring the Steelers to thump the Colts 28–10. The legend of the Terrible Towel was born. "At first I thought it was kind of silly," said linebacker Andy Russell, "but when you look into the stands and see those towels waving and those people screaming, you start to believe." With their towel-waving fans behind them, the Steelers went on to defeat the Dallas Cowboys 21–17 in Super Bowl X. From then on, the Terrible Towel has been an essential accessory for every Steelers fan.

A MAGICAL RIDE FOR THE BUS

In 2005, the Steelers had to win their final four games to clinch the sixth and final AFC playoff spot. Winning three playoff games on the road was a tall order to fill, but this squad was on a mission to win it for "The Bus." Star running back Jerome Bettis, known affectionately as "The Bus," was nearing the end of his extraordinary 13-year career. The Steelers wanted to win a championship for their burly star, and with Super Bowl XL being played in Bettis's hometown of Detroit, Michigan, his teammates could not imagine a better place for a fitting send-off. In the playoffs, the Steelers played inspired football as they defeated the Cincinnati Bengals, Indianapolis Colts, and Denver Broncos on their charge to the Super Bowl. Facing the Seattle Seahawks in the title game, the Steelers rolled to a 21–10 victory. "I can't believe it. I am blessed," said an emotional Bettis, who retired shortly after the game. "To win a championship with these guys in front of my family and friends is like a dream come true."

Like Noll and Cowher before him, Tomlin looked to energize
the Steelers by developing the team's young talent. Rising
stars such as Roethlisberger, wide receiver Santonio Holmes,
and linebacker James Harrison sparked the 2007 Steelers to
a 10–6 record and the AFC North Division title. Then, in 2008,
behind the NFL's top-ranked defense, the Steelers went 12–4
and fought past two playoff opponents to reach the Super
Bowl, where they met the Arizona Cardinals.

Super Bowl XLIII could not have started better for the
Steelers. Roethlisberger confidently led the offense up and
down the field, and after Harrison returned an interception
100 yards for a touchdown (the longest play in Super Bowl
history), Pittsburgh led 17–7 at halftime and 20–7 in the

X Tight end Heath
Miller was valued most
for his blocking and
short-yardage catches,
but he broke loose for
an 87-yard touchdown
catch in 2006.

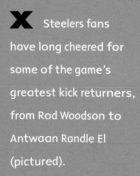

✕ Steelers fans have long cheered for some of the game's greatest kick returners, from Rod Woodson to Antwaan Randle El (pictured).

ROD WOODSON

CORNERBACK
STEELERS SEASONS: 1987-96
HEIGHT: 5-FOOT-11
WEIGHT: 205 POUNDS

One of the greatest all-around athletes ever to play in the NFL, Rod Woodson came to the Steelers after earning All-American honors in football and track at Purdue University. As Pittsburgh's first-round pick in 1987, Woodson made an immediate impact on the field as both a cornerback on defense and a kick returner on special teams. During his 10 seasons in Pittsburgh, Woodson made the Pro Bowl 7 times, snagged 38 interceptions, and returned 4 kicks for touchdowns. Opposing quarterbacks knew better than to throw to Woodson's side of the field. To lure a quarterback into challenging him, Woodson would often intentionally let a receiver appear to be open until the throw was made, then he would use his raw speed to close the gap and make the interception. Woodson was also a model of Steelers toughness. After seriously injuring his knee during the 1995 season opener, Woodson underwent major surgery and worked tirelessly to rehabilitate the injury. Later that season, when the Steelers took the field for Super Bowl XXX, Woodson was back in the lineup, ready to help his team.

third quarter. The Cardinals then surged back, scoring 16 unanswered points to take the lead. But the Steelers were not done. Late in the fourth quarter, they drove 78 yards, and Roethlisberger connected with Holmes in the back corner of the end zone with 35 seconds left to give Pittsburgh a 27–23 win. It was the Steelers' second Super Bowl victory in four years and sixth overall—more than any other team in history. "We never gave up," said Ward. "To come back and win it like that is just unbelievable."

The history of the Pittsburgh Steelers runs as long and as deep as the rivers that course through the city. Lovable losers for nearly 40 years, the Steelers rose to greatness on the strength of their hard work, talent, and iron will, and they have come to represent excellence in the NFL. With their legions of fans behind them, it likely won't be long before Pittsburgh's latest men of steel capture Super Bowl victory number seven.

One of the key leaders of the Pittsburgh defense, hard-hitting linebacker James Harrison was named the NFL's 2008 Defensive Player of the Year. **X**

INDEX